Perspectives of Nature

Perspectives of Nature
ISBN: 978-1-945307-06-5

Copyright © 2017 by Paul Košir
First published September, 2017

With the exception of brief quotes for the purpose of review, no part of this book may be reproduced or utilized in any form or by any means, electronic or mechanical, without express written permission from the publisher.

Published by
Nature Works Publishing
1235 Denton Street
La Crosse, WI 54601
sciromanticpoetry@gmail.com

Book designed by Rodney Schroeter

Perspectives of Nature

Scientifically Romantic and Experiential Nature Poetry

by Paul Košir

ACKNOWLEDGEMENTS

I must gratefully acknowledge
Rodney Schroeter,
whose confidence from the beginning
in my scientifically romantic style of poetry
made this project imaginable
and whose advice throughout the process
made the project achievable.

I also must gratefully acknowledge
the contributions to this work
of the members of the
La Crosse Area Writers Group,
who claimed no particular aptitude for poetry,
yet helped me to polish my good poems
into publishable works.

Finally, I must gratefully acknowledge
my wife, Lilly,
for her cheerful and helpful responses
to my frequent questions and complaints
while dealing ineffectively
with computer situations.

Author's Introduction

When I began writing poetry in the late 1980s, my style was already established. "The Northern Lights," "Hoar Frost," and "October Color" were scientifically romantic; "March Thaw" was experiential; and "Winter" was purely didactic. I wrote "Warblers" and "Hawk-watching" for a little bird field guide I put together in 1990, while at Wyalusing State Park.

For more than two decades, I wrote no poems. Then, early in 2012, I wrote "Sun Dogs" to see if I still had the knack. With renewed confidence in my ability, I joined the Wisconsin Writers Association and entered "The Northern Lights" in the Jade Ring contest. It won 3rd place in the formalist poetry category. The next year it was one of four poems of mine to appear in the anthology, *A Wisconsin Harvest, Volume 2*, published by the WWA Press.

In 2016, I was approached by Rodney Schroeter about publishing a booklet of my poems with scientific themes, and *Perspectives of Nature* was born.

Most of the poems in this booklet have scientific themes and many of them use scientific terms. Definitions of more obscure terms and infrequently-used words can be found on the left-hand page opposite the poem in which the words or terms are used. These include terms that have more familiar definitions in contexts other than science (e.g. "kettle" and "cones"). Readers who are not well grounded in the subject matter of particular poems are encouraged to make use of the definitions on the left-hand pages. They are listed in order of appearance in the associated poem.

Readers who purchase print editions of this booklet may want to use the blank portions of the left-hand pages for journal entries. Such entries could be as simple as recording when and where events described in the poems are observed. Or they could include detailed information about the events: time of day, weather conditions, individuals present, descriptions, and emotional responses. These pages also could be used to record notes and observations in any of the various topics found in the poems. Making syrup, honey bee activity, groundhog predictions, locations of glacial features, and the progression of fall color are all worthy entries.
Writing in this booklet would not ruin its leaves, but cause them to flower.

I invite you to enjoy this poetry by reading and re-reading it, then sharing it with others, perhaps even reading or reciting favorite poems when appropriate. May the poetry found herein enlighten and inspire all who read or hear it.

— P. K.
September, 2017

Dedication

To Lilly,

who's always been supportive wife
in my not-always-normal life.

Table of Contents

Acknowledgements iv
Author's Introduction v
Snow Flakes 1
Hoar Frost 3
Hail 5
Earth's Gifts 7
Rainbow 9
Sun Dogs 11
Sunset 13
The Northern Lights 15
Meteors 17
Eclipses 19
Earth 21
Caves 23
Life's History 25
Warmth 27
October Color 29
Winter 31
Groundhog Day 33
February, February Too 35
March Thaw 37
Syrup 39
Honey 41
Bird Song 43
Warblers 45
Hawk-watching 47
The Sighting 49
Hummingbird Trap 51
Backwater Battle 53
Tree Fall 55
Campfire 57
Ice-Age Impact 59
Driftless Area 61
Tornado 63
Index 65
About the Author 67
Photo Credits 68

Hexag'nal (a poetic contraction of "hexagonal")
　　Six sided.

Tatting
　　Making lace

Perspectives of Nature

SNOW FLAKES

Nature, with Her molecules
of water vapor, pure and clear,
coats the tiny, glistening jewels
that build a fragile chandelier.

Forming crystals delicate,
embracing with hexag'nal arms
frozen shapes most intricate,
adorned with finest feathered charms.

Nature's patterns, ne'er seen twice,
Her art in bonds of atoms pent,
interlacing threads of ice,
Her tatting is magnificent.

Glass-like sculptures drift in air
and gently flurry as they fall,
nestle on the Earth to share
a blanket white of snowflakes small.

Notes

Rime
    Frost formed from a cloud or fog, hoar-frost.

Perspectives of Nature

HOAR FROST

Nature's silver frosting forms
in winter fog at night,

reflecting from the shrouded moon
a muted glistening light,

which pierces through the veiling cloak
to make the darkness bright.

In stillness, cooling moisture helps
the fragile rime accrue

as midnight's chill the vapors touch
to freeze the morning dew.

From icy wisps of silent air
the frozen prisms grow,

pure water from the misty clouds
shapes crystals into snow

that unseen falls upon the twigs
and feathers boughs with white.

Notes

Anvil
   The often anvil-shaped top of a cumulonimbus (storm) cloud.

Supercool
   Cool below the freezing point, possible under certain atmospheric conditions.

Perspectives of Nature

HAIL

When storm clouds reach the greatest height, their anvils in cold air,
strong updrafts rise through warm and moist; and downdrafts form a pair.
The atmospheric stage is set for Nature's juggling show,
its to-and-fro beyond our sight, we only see what's low.
The drops updrafted high enough will supercool and freeze;
these frozen orbs may fall to Earth, the size of smallest peas.
Some falling ice balls melt a bit then rise and freeze again,
which adds once more to bobbing spheres a glaze of ice so thin.
Quick-freezing layers capture air, make cloudy the veneer,
solidifying slowly and the coating's crystal clear.
The more that Nature juggles hail, the larger it will grow,
and faster must the updrafts be, to larger ice balls throw.
The unseen show lets curtain fall, the raining water dries,
replaced instead by hailing stones, a brief, imperiling prize.
Once danger's passed, we marvel at the fallen, juggled hail,
stones Mother Nature could not toss, but did She really fail?

Notes

Condensation nuclei ("*NUKE-lee-eye*")
Minute particles on which water vapor can condense to form cloud droplets.

Freezing nuclei
Minute crystalline particles on which water droplets can freeze.

Perspectives of Nature

EARTH'S GIFTS

Clouds

When water vapor in the air, as much as it can hold,
strikes condensation nuclei, minute and freezing cold,

the drops that form and bits of ice composing clouds are buoyed,
suspended by slight drafts of air till currents are destroyed.

If coldness follows humid days, clouds blossom down below,
evoke awed scenes from mountaintops, then through the valleys flow.

The cotton clouds of afternoons with crisp blue summer skies
stitch puffy shapes we cannot touch, but see in our minds' eyes.

Rain

The tiny drops in colder clouds touch freezing nuclei
then grow to snow or melt to rain and fall down from the sky.

Large droplets in the warmer clouds collide and coalesce,
to fall as rain from thunderclouds, as downpours, nonetheless.

The raging storms in Summer's heat from moisture held aloft
become in Autumn all-day rains of drizzle, calm and soft,

then change to flakes in blizzard snows, increasing Winter's drifts,
that melt and sprinkle rain in Spring upon Earth's growing gifts.

Notes

Retina
: The layer of light-sensitive tissue in the eye

Cones
: The photo-receptive cells of the eye that perceive color.

Chromatic
: Having color, especially bright colors.

Perspectives of Nature

RAINBOW

As sunlight from behind begins to shine on distant rain,
the drops refract returning light and color its refrain.
The water beads as prisms act to bend the light from Sun
and separate the spectral hues that once were found in one.

On back of spheres the shades reflect and exit opposite
to bring the picture to our eyes, where images are lit.
Our retinas in rear of eyes have different colored cones,
each sends a message to the mind, which blends and sets the tones.

Chromatic bands in misty arch appear at certain height
above, beside, around the point where viewer blocks the light.
Projected on cascading rain, a moving, steady screen,
as tall and wide as sunlit sky, yet picture briefly seen.

More fleeting, dimmer, rarer still, is higher second bow;
its drops reflect an extra time, inverting color row.
No two who view this lucky sight see rays that are the same,
which makes unique the portrait seen and memory in mind's frame.

Notes

Welkin
  Sky, upper air.

Rune
  A marking of mysterious or magical significance.

Quarter quarter
  One-sixteenth

Parhelion (*"par-HEE-lee-un"*)
  A luminous, sometimes colorful spot 22° from the Sun on each side.

Sol (*"sole"*)
  Our Sun.

Perspectives of Nature

SUN DOGS

Wispy cirrus clouds of height
at times hold ice for bending light
to form a ring-like welkin rune,
circumscribing Sun or Moon.
Each halo 'round the Sun is nigh,
at quarter quarter of the sky;
its plate-shaped crystals, left and right,
hold spectral colors, focus light,
and on each flank do mock the Sun
as dazzling parhelion.

The horizontal ice white trails
show sun dogs holding out their tails,
at heel along the sides of Sol;
their brilliant beauty plays no role,
yet always dogged suns portend
precipitation will descend.

Notes

Perspectives of Nature

SUNSET

The canvas used for sunset art
is scattered blue, from light,

that penetrates and permeates
at atmospheric height.

As it nears the Earth's horizon,
the Sun emits its beams

through longer path of atmosphere,
impeding short blue streams.

The palette used for sunset art
has longer orange and pink

to dab on clouds around the Sun
till colors start to sink.

First, purple colors tops of clouds,
which quickly slip to gray.

The canvas clears and people sleep
till sunrise comes next day.

Notes

Ion ("*EYE-on*")
   An atom or group of atoms that has lost or gained one or more electrons.

Empyreal ("*em-PURR-ee-ul*")
   Relating to the visible heavens.

Solar flare
   A short-lived outburst of solar material releasing enormous amounts of energy.

Aurora Boreal ("*aw-ROAR-uh BORE-ee-ul*")
   Aurora Borealis; the Northern Lights.

Perspectives of Nature

THE NORTHERN LIGHTS

When God, in Mother Nature's guise,
sheds Her grace upon the skies,

She magnetizes ions aerial,
preparing firmament empyreal

so that each lofty atom shines
along the Earth's magnetic lines,

in pulsing, starlit choreography,
handwritten there in bright calligraphy.

While brushing hues above the air
by virtue of a solar flare,

She weaves Her light rays into tapestry,
unveiling meteoric artistry

by drawing draperies of light
across the northern polar night,

illuminating skies ethereal,
aglow with rare Aurora Boreal.

Notes

Ion ("*EYE-on*")
    An atom or group of atoms that has lost or gained one or more electrons.

Radiant
    The point in the heavens from which meteors appear to originate.

Perspectives of Nature

METEORS

Earth's orbit intercepts the path
left by a comet's tail,

whose rock, dust, ice, and ion gas
produce a glowing trail

when entering Earth's atmosphere,
where they encounter drag

that lights the speeding molecules,
stressed by the ones that lag.

The streaks of light ephemeral
bedazzle conscious mind,

but focusing a moment late
frustrates one as if blind.

Ubiquitous, yet personal,
radiant are the showers.

Shared glimpses of a falling star
are deeper felt than flowers.

Notes

Accrete
: Increase in size by a series of additions.

Penumbra ("*pee-NUM-bra*")
: The part of the shadow of Earth or the Moon in which sunlight is partially blocked.

Umbra
: The part of the shadow of Earth or the Moon in which sunlight is fully blocked.

Maria ("*MAH-ree-uh*")
: Plural of mare, the "seas" found on the moon, which are flat, dark plains.

Sol ("*sole*")
: Our Sun.

Baily's Beads
: The "beads" of sunlight shining between the moon's mountains when a solar eclipse is near totality, first explained exactly by Francis Baily in 1836.

Shadow bands
: Undulating wavy bands of light and dark shone on plain, light-colored surfaces just before and after a total solar eclipse.

Perspectives of Nature

ECLIPSES

Cooling gas and dust in space
did long ago accrete
to form the planets 'round the Sun
and make the Earth complete.

The Moon was formed at later time,
its orbit an ellipse,
and, when aligned with Earth and Sun,
occasions an eclipse.

Lunar

First seen is faint penumbra
of copper-colored light,
followed by Earth's silhouette,
the umbra, black as night.

Earth's shadow, cast upon full Moon,
creeps 'cross the lunar face,
extinguishing the maria,
which vanish in black space.

Solar

The unseen orb of newest Moon
eclipses solar light,
when totally obscuring Sol,
it turns the day to night.

Moon's mountains Baily's Beads create
along the crescent Sun,
show shadow bands of light and dark
and twinkle then are done.

Notes

Sentience (*SEN-tee-ens*)
   Perception by the senses.

Corporeal ("*CORE-pore-EE-ul*")
   Relating to the bodily or physical realm.

Perspectives of Nature

EARTH

Inside my Mother Earth, I feel my senses go away:
no sight, no sound, no touch, no taste; my sentience does not stay.

As I descend, the light grows dim, my sight begins to gray
till blackness strikes my eyes so deep, there's nothing where I lay.

The sounds of life above persist, but not so where I rest;
the chamber walls are silent, in their stillness I am blest.

The air beyond turns still below, within my Mother's breast;
while sheltered here, I fail to feel my limbs that once were stressed.

Through muted lips do I perceive no sweet, no salt, no sour;
the only taste is bitterness of food from my last hour.

No longer can my nose provide the fragrance of a flower,
for scent is barely issued from these walls severe and dour.

The vault that holds my earthly self is not for me a grave.
Immobile, not inanimate, I'm willing, not a slave.

This meditation, now complete, my consciousness does save;
my corporeal self, serene, now bonded, leaves the cave.

Notes

Aquifer ("*AH-kwi-fer*")
A layer of saturated rock storing significant quantities of water.

Carbon's oxide gas
Carbon dioxide (CO_2), which reacts with water to form carbonic acid.

Sinkholes
Depressions in surface limestone layers that lead into caverns.

Karst
A landscape characterized by the presence of limestone caves.

Straws
Thin-walled hollow formations through which water drips, often called "soda straws."

Helictites ("*hel-LICK-tites*")
Cave formations formed from water that seeps into caves through pores and cracks rather than from dripping water, thereby allowing horizontal, curved and flat formations.

Rimstone dams
Fragile vertical walls found in cave pools.

Perspectives of Nature

CAVES

Formation

Precipitation infiltrates, fills bedrock cracks and pores,
creating rain-fed aquifers that form our water stores.

The saturated rock beneath the water table top
Reacts with carbon's oxide gas, makes acid drop by drop.

The acid weak needs Father Time to help it do its task,
so ages hence the holes are carved in Mother Nature's mask.

If water in a nearby stream erodes its bed enough,
it draws the water table down and makes the landscape rough.

The limestone rock, dissolved away, leaves sinkholes in the ground;
when deeper valleys drain the rock, then caverns will be found.

Formations

The caves so formed in regions karst build artwork where they drip,
precipitating calcium in crystals at the tip.

In humid caves the moisture dries at pace of Father Time
to build and slowly decorate the sculptures most sublime.

Straws hold evaporating drops, grow downward ring by ring,
then form, if blocked, stalactite cones that from the ceiling cling.

If water trickles down the cone, then other shapes will grow:
draperies, shawls, and bacon strips are made from stone-like flow.

Stalagmites grow in counter-sense, up from the drips that fall,
and leave their lime on growing mounds for eons small to tall.

Without a drop, helictites form from moisture in a pore;
'tis delicate, fantastic art, yet fragile to its core.

Clear, gentle streams within the caves, if blocked by rimstone dams,
have pools in which cave pearls can grow, much rarer than from clams.

Notes

Punctuations
Periods of geologically rapid evolutionary change.

Sedimentation
Deposited minerals that become rock and organic material that becomes fossils.

Perspectives of Nature

LIFE'S HISTORY

The hardest things in Life are ne'er forgotten,
they're set for the ages and written in stone:

the strength that suffuses a primitive shell,
the framework supporting Life cut to the bone

are clues to the mysteries unfolded in Life,
posterity left in impressions of yore,

punctuations engraved in layers of rock,
a record of Life as it's lived at its core.

Yet daily existence and struggles in life,
actions and instincts in Nature's creation,

learning in offspring and tending by parents
occur without trace in sedimentation.

Earth publishes not what living things utter,
their unnoted thoughts are forgotten and dead.

The soft parts of Life are all in the Present,
imbued with their genes for the Future ahead.

Notes

Metabolic heat
The heat resulting from biochemical reactions of life, animal heat.

Perspectives of Nature

WARMTH

In Autumn, shorter, cooler days
stir changes in the eating ways

of mammals who must often eat
to warm with metabolic heat.

While some continue on this road,
the finding-food-when-hungry mode,

a never-ending way of life
of feasting mixed with starving strife,

some species burrow underground
and wait for Spring to come around.

Some of the bats and many birds,
a butterfly and hoof-ed herds

migrate to find the better climes
to spend their hungry winter times.

As mammals, humans do the same.
As spirits, humans need a flame,

which friends and family help to light
to keep away the cold at night.

Some people hibernate or fly
to keep their bodies warm and dry,

but miss the visits, kith and kin,
the chance to feel, to talk and grin.

Yes, Autumn is the time of year
to build up warmth and gather cheer.

Notes

Quotes from Frost, Robert. "Nothing Gold Can Stay." *The Poetry of Robert Frost*. New York: Holt, Rinehart and Winston Inc., 1969. 222-223. Print.

Xanthophyll ("*ZAN-tho-fill*")
  Yellow pigment involved in the photosynthetic process.

Perspectives of Nature

OCTOBER COLOR

"Nature's first green is gold," writes Frost,
"Her hardest hue to hold."

For Summer hides the golden hue,
but Autumn makes it bold.

In summer leafage, Life is green
till shorter days turn chill

Then chlorophyll gives up the ghost,
revealing xanthophyll.

The red that's seen in autumn leaves
was not before produced,

Nor always shows the scarlet hue
when green becomes reduced.

As sugar forms and thriving wanes,
vermilion shades are built.

Bright sun, with its opponent cold,
the leaves do crimson gilt.

Notes

Rutting
: The behavior displayed by deer "in the rut," a period of sexual excitement and activity.

Raptors
: Birds of prey: hawks, falcons, owls, and eagles.

Perspectives of Nature

WINTER

Winter beginning Arctic air winning
Noon sun sinking Day length shrinking
Night air chilling Hoarfrost killing
Bucks end their rutting Burrow doors shutting

Sun not warming Blizzard forming
Clouds stalling Snow falling
Wind blowing Drifts growing
Mammals hiding Raptors biding

Thaw only teasing Water still freezing
Night skies clearing Cold wave nearing
Wind chill gripping Frostbite nipping
Temperature dropping Bird feeders hopping

Arctic air losing Bears finish snoozing
Days longer Sun stronger
Ice going Sap flowing
Cold diminishing Winter finishing

Notes

Vernal
  Of or relating to Spring.

Candlemas
  The Feast of the Presentation of the Lord, February 2.

Torpor ("*TORE-per*")
  Dormancy during hibernation.

Perspectives of Nature

GROUNDHOG DAY

Three hundred sixty days a year, plus four and sometimes five,
woodchucks are not that often seen and rarely seen alive.

The few who see 'chucks in the wild consider them a pest,
except on Feb the second, when they run their weather test.

'Chucks claim the name of "groundhog" then, which grants them god-like traits:
prognosticating climate and predicting vernal dates.

By legend, groundhogs leave their dens, each checking if it's made
a terrorizing silhouette or other scary shade.

If frightened, they return to hide from Winter six weeks more;
if Sun's not out, there's early Spring in shy of six weeks four.

On Candlemas the groundhogs played this shadow-boxing game
till one, because of local press, achieved the greatest fame.

Punxsutawney Phil is roused from hibernating slumber,
and asked, while still half-frozen, for the weeks of winter's number.

Most groundhogs end their torpor one month later in the wild,
but winter-weary folks can't wait for weather that is mild.

Notes

Blue Moon
   The second occasion in a calendar month of a full moon, a phase which occurs about every 29½ days.

Perspectives of Nature

FEBRUARY

The shortest month?
Hah! That's a laugh!
Each frozen day
seems one, plus half.

FEBRUARY, TOO

In February, lips turn blue,
a month too short for Moon to do.

Notes

Perspectives of Nature

MARCH THAW

I heard it one day
from the shore of the lake,

while my eyes were asleep
and my ears were awake.

I heard something happen,
so I know it was true,

and yet, oh so quiet,
like the sound of the dew.

Then, by straining my ears,
I could hear the sound more;

'twas a thunderous crash
and a deafening roar.

Though it couldn't be seen
and it couldn't be felt,

when I harkened to Spring,
I could hear the ice melt.

Notes

Phloem ("*FLOW-em*")
    The vascular tissue that conducts the sugars and other products of photosynthesis from the leaves to the roots of plants.

Xylem ("*ZYE-lem*")
    The vascular tissue that conducts water and some nutrients from the roots to the stems and leaves of plants.

Perspectives of Nature

SYRUP

While frosty morns are warmed by day
and sunny days at night turn cold,
the life of trees begins to flow
and maples pump their liquid gold.

A year before, their leaves did catch
the strength of Sun, the breath of air
to fuel the trees' life-giving sap,
stored underground for Winter bare.

Descended through the phloem tubes
in Summer's growth and Autumn's fall,
life rested Winter under snow,
rising back through xylem tall.

In early Spring, when frozen trees
begin to thaw in mildest heat,
some tap the flowing life dilute,
distilling from it something sweet.

Notes

Forage bees
: The bees that forage for nectar, pollen, and water.

Enzyme
: A protein acting as a catalyst in a biochemical reaction.

Hexagon-al
: Six sided.

Royal jelly
: Secretion from worker bee glands that is fed to the queen and all young bees.

Drones
: Male bees that do no work and have the sole purpose of mating with the queen.

Perspectives of Nature

HONEY

I pet a bee whene'er I dare, I try not to recoil,
for in this clumsy way I try to thank her for her toil.

I watch the workers, one by one, across the meadow fly;
the forage bees have said with dance that there the flowers lie.

Some flowers' petals guide the bees and show them where to light
to gather nectar from each bloom, and pollen, dry and bright.

With baskets full of pollen food, they make a bee-line back,
the nectar sipped by worker bees still held in special sac.

By work of mouth an enzyme turns the nectar each bee brings,
to honey thin that next is fanned as workers flap their wings.

The thickened sweet is stored in combs of hexagon-al cells
and capped with wax for winter food, creating honey wells.

The royal jelly's made and fed three days to all young bees,
but on and on to larvae crowned "queen mother," if you please.

By mating with the male drones, establishing her brood,
she gives them life, then I can share their produce and their food.

Notes

Henslow's
   Henslow's sparrow.

Syrinx ("*SEAR-inks*")
   The vocal organ of birds, located at the fork of the trachea (windpipe).

Perspectives of Nature

BIRD SONG

In order to communicate, birds utter different calls,
a lexicon of notes in life as told through phonic scrawls.

Their sweeter songs have other goals; each male sings in his realm
to shoo the other males away, woo females from the helm.

Her response to avian ads will carry on her race,
yet in her choice, she may begin a dialect of place.

The lyrics crooned by vying males are sung distinctively;
while judging features of each bird, she rates him on his plea.

The longest and most intricate from tiny winter wren,
just a hiccup from the Henslow's as he wobbles to his den.

Most curious from bobolink – the oingo boingo bird –
yet even more unusual when two at once are heard.

A thrush sings with both syrinx sides, a different pitch in each,
making flute-like and ethereal the lonesome male's beseech.

These mimic thrushes copy snips from songs of other birds:
grey catbirds once, brown thrashers twice, and mockingbirds do thirds.

More than a song from sandhill cranes, their courtship is a dance:
males rub on mud then bugle mates to intimately prance.

Notes

Perspectives of Nature

WARBLERS

They never stop moving, I can't get a good look;
when they finally sit perched, it's not like in the book.

All seem to be yellow and they look just the same,
so the hardest thing yet is to call each by name.

And their warbling songs are no treat to my ears;
the sneaks hide behind leaves then taunt me with jeers.

I'll look in the tree tops, that's the best place to check;
that'll prove that all warblers are a pain in the neck!

Notes

Perspectives of Nature

HAWK-WATCHING

Whenever I gawk,
I see a big hawk

that's almost too high
to see with my eye.

I wish it would perch
right here in this birch

and tell me its name
to settle this game.

Notes

Perspectives of Nature

THE SIGHTING

An owl appeared and glided to a river bottom tree
and landed on the outer edge, a place that I could see.

It held its branch and looked for food upon the forest floor.
My view so good, the sight so rare, I watched a little more.

There were two tufts atop its head, but not where ears did grow;
they're buried deep in facial discs, one higher up, one low.

Such ears allow an owl at night to find whate'er it hears,
including noises under snow, and by those sounds it steers.

As well as sound, the facial discs can gather in scant light,
perceived by oddly-shaped large eyes as something almost bright.

Its eyes so big, they cannot move, an owl must turn its head,
from part-way rear and side to side, three-fourths around the spread.

With special fringing on its wings, an owl flies silently,
which helps it sneak up on its prey and kill it instantly.

Its perfect camouflage can help an owl avoid a stare.
The owl appeared and glided in, but then it wasn't there.

Notes

Perspectives of Nature

HUMMINGBIRD TRAP

The smallest bird I'd ever seen, its back and wings metallic green,
ensnared within a monstrous trap with, at one end, enormous gap,
held hostage by the thought ingrained that flying up is freedom gained.
Without delay and not a word, I raised a staff to help the bird.
On end it perched repeatedly; I dipped the pole to set it free.
Each time it got near open space, it flew to roof board closed-in place.
The hummingbird began to fade, once buzzing past, it now was staid.
The little bird had little time; with bag in hand, I made my climb.
Ascending to within arm's length, I saw the hummer losing strength.
I slowly reached out with my hand to catch what now could barely stand.
Through porous bones I felt its heart, its tiny, racing, living part.
With lightest touch, I held the life that on each front found danger rife.
I gently placed it in the sack, crawled 'round the rafter beam and back
to shaky ladder down I crept while female ruby-throated slept.
When finally down upon the Earth, I ope'd the pouch and gave rebirth.
It flew to food, red blossoms fair, and from garage, the man-made snare.

Notes

Perspectives of Nature

BACKWATER BATTLE

I saw the struggle, life and death,
a savagery that took my breath.
One fiercely fought, its life to save,
on every gently flowing wave.
It thrashed and took an upstream tack,
the fish snake-bitten on its back.
The snake and fish, with raging might,
swam in their fury out of sight.
The rivals soon in weakened state
succumbed to river current fate.
Descending past, the bitter foes
dragged out their drama toward its close.
The perch could not its burden shake
nor predatory death-grip break.
The water snake persisted more,
yet river washed them both ashore.

Notes

Happed
    Happened by chance.

Perspectives of Nature

TREE FALL

I led our fleet that gifted day
along the river's shore.
Our canoes divided water,
my vessel in the fore.
As was my wont, I talked a while
before we paddled more.
'Tween islands lush we moved our boats
as many times before.
But this time came a thing so rare,
it added to my lore.
I knew not what would happen
nor what was for us in store.

This common, rarely-seen event
happed with no human hand:
the oldest tree before our eyes
fell over to the land.

Notes

Ion ("*EYE-on*")
   An atom or group of atoms that has lost or gained one or more electrons.

Perspectives of Nature

CAMPFIRE

The air is crisp, the tinder dried,
the fuel is set, combustion tried.

Tinder for a camping fire ignites imagination,
ere the match is even struck burns bright anticipation.

The twigs arranged in kindling pyre
like dominoes will fall to fire.

Puffing glowing sparks to flames prevents the fire from waning;
the heat-dry-fuel-and-oxygen reaction starts sustaining.

More wood creates a bigger blaze
with flickered light to hold our gaze.

Though dancing flames of ion gas seem not to be substantial,
this element from ancient times still is consequential.

Our fire, less stoked, burns down to coals
to meet marshmallow-roasting goals.

Its glowing embers in our eyes connect us with the Past,
when roasting-boiling-warming fires for living had to last.

Notes

Firn
Granular snow that has survived a summer melting season and will become glacial ice.

Erratic
A glacially-transported rock that is unlike the rocks where it was deposited.

Kettle
A depression in glacial drift caused by an ice mass.

Kame
Steep-sided mound of glacial deposits.

Drift
Any sediment associated with the action of glacial ice.

Moraine ("*more-AIN*")
Material deposited along the side or end of a glacier.

Esker
Long, sinuous hill made up of sand and gravel deposits of a sub-glacial river.

Drumlin
Tear drop-shaped landform, blunt on one end and tapered in the direction of ice flow.

Till
Sediments laid down by direct action of glacial ice without water present.

Perspectives of Nature

ICE-AGE IMPACT

When snows outlast the summer's heat, the flakes begin to turn
from fluffy white, compressed by weight, to grainy ice called firn.

As snowball squeezed by throwing hand refreezes and compacts,
snow on a continental scale forms massive frozen tracts.

The buildup over Canada, piled high beyond belief,
above the southern Hudson Bay, was two miles in relief.

The weight of this enormous sheet forced glacial ice to spread
so snow pack in the northern states continued to be fed,

And on this front, ice left its mark with features that it formed
on landscapes north across the land, as frozen water warmed.

When climates changed and ice withdrew, the snows replaced by rains,
they inundated, sculpted dells and leveled outwash plains.

The tidal flood of melting frost, erratics in its wake,
left kettles filled with frozen bergs that warmed to flood each lake.

The water pooled atop the mass, drawn off as if by drain,
built hill-like kames of glacial drift that settled grain by grain.

Like ice cube dropped on sandy beach, each massive glacier lobe
had drift on edge and thawed to leave moraines linked round the globe.

Beneath enormous slab of ice flowed water freezing cold,
precipitating drift that helped curved eskers fill the mold.

With no one there to see the way that drumlins got their shape,
by adding or subtracting till, 'tis hid behind Time's drape.

Ice spread around a drumlin's core to make its front edge shear
then smoothed the mound of glacial till to leave a drumlin tear.

Notes

Drift
Any sediment associated with the action of glacial ice.

Till
Sediments laid down by direct action of glacial ice without water present.

Loess ("*less*")
Sediments deposited by the wind.

Karst
A landscape characterized by the presence of limestone caves.

Rill
A small stream.

Dendritic ("*den-DRIT-ick*")
Tree-like, especially in pattern of branching.

Relict pines
Pine forests in the Driftless Area that have persisted since glaciation ended.

Contour farms
Farms that grow crops in rows on the level across or perpendicular to slopes.

Perspectives of Nature

DRIFTLESS AREA

A dry plateau in sea of ice
was spared from glacial action twice

and twice again evaded weight
of glaciers huge, with impact great.

The isolation of the land
let rare, endangered species stand.

No drift or till ice carried in,
yet wind-blown loess again, again.

Where glaciers crept, they filled each cave,
but landscapes karst did Driftless save.

With sediments from river laid
and ice-age features never made,

the force that shaped the Driftless Zone?
Erosion carved the Earth, alone.

The valleys cleft by rill and stream,
adjoined above by ridge-top seam,

intersect as twig to limb,
dendritic flow to sea from rim.

This water drain impounds no lake,
but floodplains flat create a brake

in wetlands 'long the river shore,
where glacial outwash formed a floor.

A host of bluffs and relict pines,
man's contour farms, historic mines

are found throughout the Driftless Lands,
some made by God, some, human hands.

Notes

Perspectives of Nature

RENDING ROOFS & WRECKING HOMES
DESTRUCTION LEFT BEHIND
WRENCHING HEARTS
& ROBBING REST
DESTROYING
PEACE OF
MIND
TOR
NA
D
O

Index

About the Author 67
Acknowledgements iv
Author's Introduction v
Backwater Battle 53
Bird Song 43
Campfire 57
Caves 23
Driftless Area 61
Earth 21
Earth's Gifts 7
Eclipses 19
February, February Too 35
Groundhog Day 33
Hail 5
Hawk-watching 47
Hoar Frost 3
Honey 41
Hummingbird Trap 51
Ice-Age Impact 59
Index 65
Life's History 25
March Thaw 37
Meteors 17
October Color 29
Photo Credits 68
Rainbow 9
Snow Flakes 1
Sun Dogs 11
Sunset 13
Syrup 39
The Northern Lights 15
The Sighting 49
Tornado 63
Tree Fall 55
Warblers 45
Warmth 27
Winter 31

About the Author

The scientifically romantic nature poetry of Paul Košir has its academic roots in his nine years as a student at the University of Wisconsin-Madison. There he earned bachelor's degrees in math, natural science, and history. In 2010 he received a master's degree in natural resources and environmental education from UW-Stevens Point.

The experiential poetry was drawn from his twelve years as the naturalist at Wyalusing State Park near Prairie du Chien, Wisconsin. He also drew on this background to write articles for *Wisconsin Natural Resources* and *La Crosse Magazine* and to publish the book *Wyalusing History*.

Košir has taught biology, physical science, and math at the high school level; and earth science, biology, and environmental issues at the college level. As a naturalist, he taught all ages about nature through hikes, programs, and displays, something he still does occasionally as a volunteer.

Born in Milwaukee, Košir now lives in La Crosse with his wife and their two sons. He enjoys learning, writing, hiking, bird-watching, gardening, traveling, and working on the family's 13 acres in the Driftless Area near Hillsboro, Wisconsin.

Photo credits:

Front cover: Author's son in Hillsboro township, Wisconsin.

Back cover: Author's son on Clingman's Dome,
Great Smoky Mountains National Park.

Both photos taken by the author,
and Copyright © 2017 by Paul Košir.

Tornado photo:
This photo was taken by participants during official,
federally funded field research programs, and is in the public domain.
Photo courtesy of NOAA's National Severe Storms Laboratory.
Taken June 2, 1995, South of Dimmitt, Texas.

www.ingramcontent.com/pod-product-compliance
Lightning Source LLC
Chambersburg PA
CBHW071540080526
44588CB00011B/1734